Movable Bean Feasts

100 plus Interesting and Easy Vegetarian Recipes

by

Charlie Davis

GW00705967

Editions de la
Montagne

Published by

Editions de la

/\\ontagne

PO Box 732
Southampton
SO16 7RQ
England
©2000 EdlM

ISBN 0 9533386 2 2

...we could go on ... but heck, take a gamble, buy the book and let's cook instead!!

This book is dedicated to the many friends who have suffered my cooking and have lived to tell the tale

Grateful thanks are also due to Adèle for her usual dedication and hard work and Marilyn for her appraisal and encouragement

He's still lying about the friends - the garlic proved too much!!
- Ed.

Origination by EdlM
Printed by IHDP

i

Foreword

The main intention of this book, like that of its companion

is to show what can be achieved with the least equipment and lowest cost.

* The recipes are basic and easy since most are also intended for quick preparation with the minimum of fuss. Nevertheless, many are quite unusual!

* Most of the ingredients are readily available but several are not vital so don't worry if you lack something. Substitute! How do you think I learned to cook! It is not (usually) fatal!

* Quantities are not critical and are volumetric rather than weight-based to avoid the need for weighing if you are camping for example

* Scale up / down quantities according to the number of lucky diners or their appetites!

* All peelable items apart from potatoes in jackets and perhaps tomatoes are assumed to be peeled! Similarly, cans and packets are to be opened, pips and stones to be removed and vegetables to be washed! Need I say more? (Apart from reminding you to take off plastic wrapping?)

* If you don't like cooking with wine, drink it instead - it will improve the meal no end!

* Garlic isn't compulsory! - but remember the Mediterranean adage: "He who has eaten garlic cannot tell whether his companion has."

* (and it keeps away werewolves and predatory landlords - handy if in a tent or digs!)

Contents

page

Symbols

Ingredients

Method

Approximate cooking time   e.g. 15 mins   1 hour

Utensils

Pan as available - frying pan, saucepan, mess tin

Number of burners

Number of people

Barbecue

Grill

Bowl / heatproof dish

Additional pot and burner for rice etc if available

The bare minimum of utensils and heat sources is given. If you have more, use them if you want!

Asparagus and Chicory Grill

1 can of asparagus spears drained
2 small chicory spears
½ cup olive oil
2 cloves garlic crushed
grated peel and juice of ½ lemon
1 tablespoon basil chopped
½ mug Cheddar or Parmesan grated
salt and pepper

Boil the chicory for a few minutes until just softening. Drain and place with asparagus in a heatproof dish. Mix oil, juice, peel, garlic and basil and pour over vegetables. Grill for 5 minutes, add cheese and grill for a further 5 minutes or until golden.

Baked Beans Improved

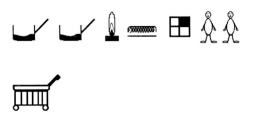

1 large can baked beans in tomato sauce
½ mug grated Cheddar
2 thick slices of bread toasted - preferably wholemeal granary
2 knobs butter
1 medium onion chopped
Worcestershire sauce
salt and pepper
peanuts

Fry the onion until transparent whilst beans are heating and toast
is grilling. Butter toast, spoon on beans and top with onion and
grated cheese. Add a few drops of sauce, salt and pepper. Scatter
a few salted roast peanuts.

Baked Beans Improved Out of All Recognition

1 large can baked beans in tomato sauce
½ mug crumbled blue cheese
2 thick slices of bread toasted - preferably wholemeal granary
2 knobs butter with crushed garlic
1 medium onion chopped
2 - 4 mushrooms chopped
2 drops tabasco
a few cashew nuts or peanuts crushed
2 tablespoons red wine (students will know what this is - Ed.)
Worcestershire sauce
a sprig of fresh basil chopped
salt and pepper

Add the tabasco, wine and Worcestershire sauce to the beans.
Fry the onions and mushrooms. Heat the beans, make the toast,
butter it with the garlic butter and pour on beans. Top with basil,
onions, mushrooms, cheese and nuts.

Barbecued Spuds with Cream Sauce

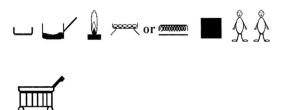

2 large potatoes scrubbed
vegetable oil
1 tablespoon white vinegar
1 bunch spring onions chopped
1 egg yolk
1 teaspoon mustard powder
1 teaspoon sage chopped
2 or 3 tablespoons thick fresh cream

Prick the potatoes and brush with oil. Wrap separately in double
foil. Grill or barbecue for about an hour or until soft. Heat onions
in vinegar until latter is almost evaporated. Remove from heat.
Beat yolk with mustard and season. Add onions and cream and
heat very gently for a minute, taking care not to turn the cream
sour. Cut a deep cross in the top of the potatoes and spoon in
dressing.

Breakfast Omelette

3 eggs
1 tomato
1 mug mushrooms chopped
2 knobs butter
a small quantity of vegetarian (soya) "bacon bits"
salt and pepper

Fry mushrooms in butter. Beat the eggs and seasoning together and pour into the hot pan. Add slices of tomato and "bacon bits," cook until set and beginning to turn golden on the base.

Broccoli Cheesebake

2 medium heads of broccoli
1 onion chopped
2 cloves garlic chopped
2 large knobs butter
2 eggs
1 small carton single cream
2-3 tablespoons Parmesan
one of the tomato sauces on pp 54 / 95
salt and pepper

Cook broccoli in boiling water for 8 minutes and cut up in largish
pieces. Drain well. Fry onion, garlic and broccoli for 5 minutes.
Beat eggs and cream with a fork until smooth, seasoning well.
Butter a heatproof dish and place vegetable mixture in it, pour over
the eggs and cook under the grill until almost set. Sprinkle with
Parmesan and grill for a further few minutes.

Eat with a tomato sauce as suggested.

Camembert Omelette

3 eggs
½ Camembert cheese
1 tablespoon double cream
1 mug of mushrooms sliced
1 onion (shallot preferred) finely chopped

Slice the Camembert into fairly thick slices, removing all the crust.
Fry onion with mushrooms and then put aside whilst making an
omelette. Fill the omelette with the onion / mushroom mixture and
fold over. Sprinkle with cream, cover with cheese and brown
under a very hot grill.

Celeriac Cheesebake

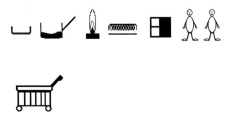

1 small celeriac cut into 6mm thick slices
2 large knobs butter
1 large block of Cheddar
2 mugs liquid crème fraîche
1 mug bread crumbs
salt and pepper

Fry the celeriac gently in butter for about 10 minutes. Add enough crème fraîche to cover the slices and cook slowly for another 15 minutes, adding more crème fraîche if required. Slice the Cheddar, butter a heatproof flat dish and put alternate layers of cheese and celeriac. Top off with a sprinkling of breadcrumbs. Put under a hot grill for 10 minutes or so.

Cheesy Eggs

2 large eggs
enough thin slices of Cheddar to cover the bread in a double layer
2 thick slices of bread - preferably wholemeal granary
1 knob butter
2 tablespoons oil
1 tablespoon sweet pickle
Worcestershire sauce

Start frying the eggs and in the meantime grill one side of the bread. Turn the bread, grill lightly, cover with cheese, a layer of sweet pickle, 2-3 drops of Worcestershire sauce and another layer of cheese. Grill until cheese melts and top with fried egg.

Cheesy Onions

2 large onions
2 slices of Cheddar cheese

Cut the onions in half, top to bottom, and place a slice of cheese between the two halves. Wrap completely in kitchen foil and cook on the barbecue or under the grill for about half an hour, turning from time to time.

Chilli Beans and Sweetcorn

1 can red kidney beans drained and washed
1 small can sweetcorn drained
1 onion chopped
1 small courgette sliced
½ red pepper chopped
2 mugs vegetable stock
4 cloves garlic crushed
½ hot chilli chopped very small
chilli powder to taste
salt and pepper

Fry the onion, garlic and pepper until soft, add the courgette and
fry for a further couple of minutes. Add the other ingredients
apart from the sweetcorn, bring to boil, cover and simmer for
30 minutes, adding the corn for the last 2 minutes.
Add more chilli during cooking if required.

Chilli Pasta

sufficient cold cooked pasta shapes for two
sweet pepper sauce
mayonnaise
2 spring onions chopped
salt and pepper

Mix pasta with a tablespoon of mayonnaise or more to taste, a teaspoon or two of sweet pepper sauce and the spring onions. Season.

Chilli, Mushroom and Beans

1 small aubergine diced
1 mug mushrooms chopped
1 onion chopped
2 cloves garlic crushed
½ teaspoon paprika
½ - 1 teaspoon cumin
1 can tomatoes or better, the equivalent fresh, chopped
1 cup vegetable stock
1 tablespoon tomato paste
1 can red kidney beans
1 tablespoon fresh coriander chopped
olive oil
salt and pepper

Fry aubergine until golden. Put aside and fry onion, garlic and spices for 5 minutes. Add tomatoes and stock and boil for 40 minutes. Add mushrooms, aubergine and tomato paste.
Drain beans and add with coriander to pan. Cook for further 20 minutes. Season and serve with rice.

Citron Rice with Vegetables

1 tablespoons lemon juice
1 tablespoons sugar
vegetable stock
1 mug long grain rice
1 cinnamon stick
2 - 3 cloves
1 knob butter
1 teaspoon cumin
1 onion finely chopped
1 small courgette
1 handful cashew nuts chopped
1 tablespoon mint freshly chopped
salt and pepper

Mix lemon juice and sugar and add 1 mug of vegetable stock, together with cloves, cinnamon, a pinch of salt and the rice. Bring to the boil and add more stock as the liquid is absorbed. Cook for ten minutes until no more stock is absorbed and remove from heat. Fry for 2 - 3 minutes the onion, cumin and courgettes with nuts and mint. Add rice and heat through.

Cold Basil and Tomato Soup

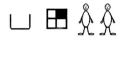

1 bunch of fresh basil finely chopped
1 tablespoon vinegar
2 tablespoons olive oil
1 can of plum tomatoes
salt and pepper
honey to taste (or sugar if honey is not available)

Chop tomatoes and mash thoroughly in their juice. Squeeze
through a sieve if you have one and mix with other ingredients.

Corsican Beans

1 pack quorn sausages
1 can white haricots
2 cloves garlic crushed
1 small goat's cheese chopped into little pieces
1 onion chopped
2 tablespoons tomato paste
thyme
1 bay leaf
olive oil
salt and pepper

Cook the sausages as instructed on the pack. Fry the onion then add the sausages, cheese, garlic, herbs and tomato paste with a tablespoon or two of water. Heat and stir well. Add to the beans and heat through. Remove the bay leaves and eat hot with crusty bread.

Cottage Cheese Omelette

4 eggs whites and yolks separated
1 knob of butter
1 small tub of cottage cheese
2 tomatoes sliced
parsley
salt and pepper

Beat the yolks lightly, add the cheese and season. In another bowl, beat the whites until stiff and then fold into the yolk and cheese mixture. Melt the butter in the pan and pour in the mixture. Cook for a minute then add the tomato slices. Cook for a further minute or two until done.

Variation:

Sprinkle with Parmesan and chopped garlic and finish off under the grill.

Crab and Sweetcorn Soup

1 can crab meat drained and flaked
1 small can sweetcorn drained
1 onion chopped
1 small courgette sliced
½ red pepper chopped
2 mugs vegetable stock
4 cloves garlic crushed
2 teaspoons plum sauce
1 teaspoon prepared ginger
1 teaspoon Hoi Sin sauce
2 teaspoons light soy sauce
pepper

Fry the vegetables in a little oil and ginger for a couple of minutes.
Stir in rest of ingredients, bring to boil and simmer for 30 minutes,
adding more stock if necessary
Season to taste.

Cress Dressing

1 small carton yogourt
1 small bunch watercress, well washed and chopped
1 dessert spoon mustard
1 small bunch spring onions or chives chopped
salt and pepper

Mix well. If you are at home and have a blender, it makes a
superb salad or pasta dressing.

Crisped Potatoes

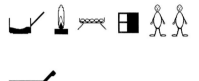

2 large potatoes scrubbed and sliced paper thin
salt
4 tablespoons sunflower oil

Plunge potato slices immediately into boiling water and stir to
separate. Leave to cook for a minute or two. Remove from water,
sprinkle with salt, roll carefully and impale on a long kebab stick,
leaving a small space between each slice. Brush with oil and cook
over barbecue, turning frequently, until crisp.

Crunchy Herb Omelette

3 eggs
3 teaspoons oil
1 knob of butter
1 slice of white bread crusts removed and cubed
½ teaspoon fresh mixed herbs
2 tomatoes chopped
2 spring onions
salt and pepper

Fry the cubes in a little very hot oil until golden and put aside. Fry the tomatoes for a minute or two until soft. Meanwhile, beat the eggs with herbs and seasoning in a bowl. Pour the mixture into the pan, add the bread cubes and cook as usual. Garnish with chopped spring onions. If preferred, add the cubes as a garnish instead of incorporating into the omelette.

Crunchy Potato Peel

2 large potatoes scrubbed
1 knob butter
salt and pepper

Wrap potatoes in foil and cook on barbecue for 45 minutes or until done. Cut lengthways and remove flesh. Save for potato salad or mash. Cut the potato skin into strips and dip into seasoned melted butter and grill on barbecue for 5 - 7 minutes.

Crunchy Salsify Omelette

3 eggs
3 teaspoons oil
1 knob of butter
1 slice of white bread crusts removed and cubed
½ teaspoon fresh mixed herbs
2 tomatoes chopped
2 spring onions chopped
a small quantity of salsify root chopped
salt and pepper

Fry the salsify slowly until cooked and turning golden.Add the rest of the vegetables and cook for a further couple of minutes. Make the omelette as usual.

Variation:

Use celeriac, carrots, red or yellow peppers instead of salsify.

Crusty Garlic Spuds

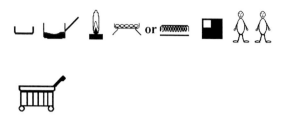

6 small new potatoes scrubbed
6 cloves garlic peeled
2 eggs beaten
3 - 4 tablespoons cornflour
parsley
salt and pepper

Boil potatoes for 15 minutes with the garlic in salted water. Drain
and keep the garlic. Peel potatoes when cool enough. Chop garlic
and insert deep into flesh of potatoes with the aid of a kebab stick
or similar. Coat potatoes in egg and flour and then again in egg.
Cook on a well oiled grill on a barbecue or under a grill for 10 - 15
minutes until crisp and golden.
Sprinkle with parsley.

Curried Eggs

4 newly hard boiled eggs chopped
2 knobs butter
2 teaspoons oil
2 large onions finely chopped
1 clove garlic finely chopped
2 tablespoons curry powder
1 tablespoon flour
1 tablespoon tomato paste
2 tablespoons chutney or sweet pickle
1 tablespoon lemon juice
3 teaspoons sugar
1½ mugs stock or water
ground ginger and cinnamon if available
salt to taste

Fry onion and garlic in oil and butter until soft. Stir in curry
 powder and flour and add tomato paste, chutney, lemon juice,
sugar and also ginger and cinnamon if used. Blend in stock or
water, add salt, bring to boil and then simmer for ¾ hour. Pour
over hard boiled eggs which are still warm.

Curried Pasta Shells

Pasta shells for 2 people - see packet for quantities
1 onion chopped
6 mushrooms chopped
1 teaspoon curry powder
1 tablespoon oil
2 teaspoons mango chutney

Cook the pasta shells and keep warm. Fry the curry powder in the oil, adding the onion and mushroom and cook until soft. Remove from the heat, stir in the mango chutney and the drained pasta shells.

Curry Omelette

3 eggs
3 teaspoons curry powder
1 onion finely chopped
1 cored diced apple
3 teaspoons mango chutney
1 teaspoon lemon juice
apple and coriander to garnish
1 knob of butter
salt and pepper

Fry onion slowly for 3 minutes and add curry powder and apple. Cook for a further five minutes then add chutney. Season and mix in lemon juice. Make omelette and fill with mixture. Fold and cut in half. Garnish as required.

Dandelion Omelette (yes you did read it correctly!)

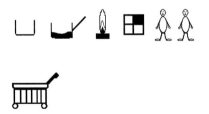

5 eggs
a quantity of young dandelion shoots chopped
2 cloves of garlic crushed
1 bunch of spring onions
1 bunch of parsley
a few drops of vinegar
some fresh herbs chopped
1 knob of butter
salt and pepper

Fry the garlic and rub around the pan. Add herbs and dandelions, sprinkle with vinegar and cook for about 5 minutes. Melt the rest of the butter and pour over beaten eggs in a bowl. Season, beat vigorously and then pour over the filling. Cook until omelette is just still runny.

Dressings - for vegetables, fish and eggs

1 tablespoon tomato paste, 1 tablespoon prepared mild (e.g. American) mustard with 1 tablespoon of light soy sauce.

2 tablespoons of crunchy peanut butter, a small onion finely chopped, a clove of chopped crushed garlic, 2 teaspoons brown sugar, 1 teaspoon lemon juice, two tablespoons of hot water with salt and pepper to taste.

1 tablespoon soy sauce, 2 teaspoons honey, 1 tablespoon pesto, 1 teaspoon dried ginger, 2 teaspoons Worcestershire sauce with 2 cloves crushed and chopped garlic.

1 tablespoon of mild prepared mustard with two tablespoons of light soy sauce and a tablespoon of grated Parmesan. Use in place of Tartare.

Salad Dressings

Chopped basil, 1 tablespoon of pine nuts, 3 tablespoons Parmesan, 1 tablespoon of white wine vinegar, 6-8 tablespoons olive oil, 2 cloves crushed garlic, pepper to taste.

5 tablespoons mayonnaise, 4 - 5 tablespoons water, 2 cloves of garlic crushed, 3 tablespoons Parmesan, salt and pepper to taste.

8 tablespoons mayonnaise, 2 teaspoons grated orange peel (without the pith), 4 teaspoons tomato paste, 2 teaspoons mild curry powder, 1 teaspoon mustard, 2 tablespoons cream, salt and pepper.

A cup of soft cheese with 4 tablespoons corn oil, 2 tablespoons lemon juice, 1 teaspoon lemon peel (without pith), ½ teaspoon mustard, salt and pepper to taste.

6 tablespoons tomato juice, 4 tablespoons olive oil, 2 tablespoons red wine vinegar, ½ teaspoon sugar and a tablespoon of chopped basil.

2 finely chopped red and yellow peppers with a clove or two of crushed garlic, 1 teaspoon paprika, ½ teaspoon mustard powder, a cup of light olive oil, salt and pepper to taste.

1 carton plain yogourt, 1 tablespoon lemon juice, 1 teaspoon honey, ½ teaspoon mustard, 4 tablespoons chopped fresh herbs.

½ mug tomato juice, ½ cup wine vinegar, 1 teaspoon grated onion, ½ teaspoon dried mustard, 1 teaspoon sugar, 1 teaspoon chopped parsley, salt and pepper.

½ cup blue cheese, ½ cup soft white cream cheese, 6 tablespoons olive oil, 1 tablespoon white wine vinegar, 1 tablespoon boiling water, salt and pepper

Dried Fruit Dressing

1 mug hazel nuts crushed
1 mug pistachios crushed
1 clove garlic crushed
1 carton mascarpone
½ teaspoon olive oil
a few dried apricots finely chopped
a few raisins and sultanas
salt and pepper

Blend nuts, fruit and mascarpone with oil. Heat very gently to reduce volume by a quarter. Season.

Eggy Bread

oil
1 - 2 eggs
2 slices of bread
salt and pepper

Beat the eggs with a little seasoning whilst heating a pan containing a couple of tablespoons of oil. Cut slices of bread into halves, dip into egg mixture and fry for a few moments.

Variations:

Use a sprinkling of your favourite herb either in the mixture or on the bread before cooking.

Sprinkle finely chopped nuts on both sides of bread before cooking.

Elba Salad

2 mugs button mushrooms
2 handfuls of green beans, fresh or frozen
1 lemon
3 tablespoons olive oil
1 lettuce heart chopped
2 cloves of garlic crushed
salt and pepper

Cook green beans, cool, drain and slice or chop. Mix the garlic
with the lemon juice, oil and seasoning. Peel the mushrooms
and cover with lemon juice to avoid blackening. Mix all
ingredients. Garnish with remaining mushrooms.

Fennel Dressing

½ fennel root
1 tablespoon celery leaves chopped
1 tablespoon lemon juice
a few drops of pastis
6 tablespoons grape seed oil
a few coriander leaves chopped (or seeds crushed)
salt and pepper

Beat salt and lemon juice, add pastis and oil, fennel, celery leaves and coriander. Mix well. Season with pepper.

Feta Salad

3 tomatoes sliced
½ cucumber sliced
1 small carton feta cheese sliced
1 bunch of basil chopped
1 tablespoon olive oil
1 lemon
a handful of black olives
a handful of unsalted peanuts
pepper

Slice cheese and marinate in olive oil, basil and pepper. Layer cheese and other ingredients to serve.

Fresh Herb Frittata

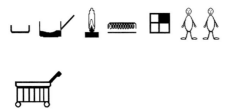

3 eggs
1 white of egg
1 medium onion chopped
1 small carton of cottage cheese
2 tablespoons fresh herbs chopped
a small quantity of rocket if available, chopped
olive oil
salt and pepper

Beat the eggs and white until well mixed, add the herbs, other
ingredients and seasoning. Cook with a little oil for 2-3 minutes
until the eggs begin to set. Put under a hot grill and leave until the
frittata turns golden.

Fruity Cheese Salad

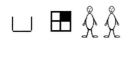

several leaves of a couple of different types of lettuce
1 chicory chopped
a small bunch each of black and white grapes halved and de-pipped
1 apple cored and chopped
a mug of cheese such as Roquefort or Danish Blue crumbled
1 bunch spring onions chopped
a dozen radishes chopped
2 teaspoons mustard powder
1 tablespoon vinegar
1 tablespoon soya oil
2 teaspoons walnut oil (if available)
salt and pepper

Wash and chop the lettuce. Blend the mustard, vinegar and oil then mix well with the salad ingredients.

Garlic Mushrooms

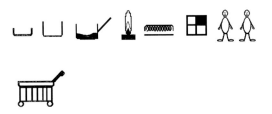

about 16 button mushrooms, whole peeled, stalks removed
2 "golf balls" of butter
2 large cloves of garlic, finely chopped
parsley, finely chopped
salt and pepper
lemon juice

Mix butter, parsley, with salt and pepper. Halve mixture and roll
one half into sausage shape and set aside. If you can, cool it.
Melt remainder and pour into mushroom cups and over stalks.
Grill for a few minutes until tender. Slice rest of mixture and place
slices on grilled mushrooms. Eat with fresh crusty wholemeal
bread to mop up butter.

Glazed Onions and Carrots

6 small carrots of about the same size whole
8 small onions whole
salt and pepper
4 - 6 tablespoons vegetable stock
2 teaspoons sugar
1 knob butter
2 teaspoons parsley chopped
salt and pepper

Boil carrots and onions in salted water for 5 - 8 minutes until soft. Drain. Heat stock, sugar and butter in pan until butter is melted and sugar dissolved. Boil briskly until volume is halved. Add vegetables and stir to coat them with glaze. Sprinkle with parsley.

Good with various quorn or tofu dishes.

Grilled Spanish Onions

2 large onions in 1cm slices
2 cloves garlic crushed
4 tablespoons double cream lightly whipped
1 tablespoon black pepper
1 knob butter
1 sprig rosemary
salt

Salt slices of onion and coat each side with cream into which
the garlic has been stirred. Add a few rosemary leaves and
a small knob of butter to each and place on a sheet of foil under
a hot grill for 5 - 8 minutes each side.

Grilled Sweetcorn with Ginger

2 corn on the cob in their leaves
2 knobs garlic butter
2 knobs of butter blended with 1 teaspoon ginger
salt and pepper

Fold back the leaves and remove the "silk" threads. Replace the leaves and soak in salt water for an hour. Drain and dry on kitchen towel. Put corn under the grill or on the barbecue until warm, remove and cover with butter. Replace and grill for 30 - 40 minutes adding butter from time to time. Season and eat at once.

Haricot and Tuna Salad

1 can of tuna in olive oil
1 can white haricots
2 cloves garlic crushed
3 sage leaves finely chopped
1 leek (white part only) chopped into rounds
salt and pepper

Break up the drained tuna and mix with other ingredients.

Haricot, Avocado and Pea Salad

1 can white haricots drained
1 avocado chopped
3 tablespoons defrosted peas
2 cloves garlic crushed
1 small goats cheese chopped into little pieces
1 onion chopped
1 tablespoon sun dried tomatoes in olive oil
1 teaspoon pesto
1 tablespoon olive oil
salt and pepper

Mix all ingredients well.

Hot Pepper Sauce

1 mug of tomato sauce
1 red and 1 green chilli chopped
1 tablespoon olive oil
salt and pepper

Fry peppers add tomato sauce and bring to boil. Allow to cool for
10 minutes. Season.

Italian Barbecued Potatoes

6 medium potatoes scrubbed
kitchen foil
2 sprigs fresh basil
1 tablespoon pesto sauce
1 tablespoon tomato paste
1 tablespoon sun dried tomatoes
2 cloves garlic crushed
1 tablespoon Worcestershire sauce
1 tablespoon Parmesan
1 teaspoon honey
salt and pepper

Bake potatoes in foil or directly over the embers for about an hour or until done. Mix the sauce ingredients and heat. Cut the potatoes lengthwise and put sauce over them.

A green salad is ideal as an accompaniment.

Italian Omelette

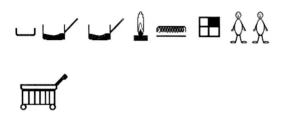

1 knob of butter
1 small onion finely chopped
1 small tomato chopped
1 tablespoon red or yellow pepper finely chopped
3 eggs
1 mug of cooked drained pasta shapes
2 tablespoons Parmesan
fresh basil if available
salt and pepper

Melt half the butter in a pan, add the onion and heat gently for a couple of minutes. Add the tomato and pepper and cook slowly for ten minutes. Beat the eggs and add pasta, salt and pepper. Melt the rest of the butter in a pan, pour in the mixture and heat gently until it just begins to set and then add the filling and fold over. Sprinkle with Parmesan and place under a hot grill until cheese melts. Cut in two, add basil and eat hot.

This omelette is also delicious cold in a sandwich of French bread.

Lawyer's Spread

4 slices of wholemeal bread
3 very ripe avocados
4 medium very ripe tomatoes
1 tablespoon mayonnaise
1 tablespoon cream cheese
1 onion
2 cloves garlic crushed
1 dash of tabasco
juice of 1 lemon or a tablespoon of ready prepared juice
several slices of cucumber
1 sprig of mint
salt and pepper

Poach tomatoes in boiling water for a couple of minutes, put into cold water and then peel. Mash the ingredients, but save a few slices of tomato and all the cucumber. Spread the bread with the mixture and place slices of tomato and cucumber on top.

Add crushed salted nuts if available, or potato crisps.

Leek and Mushroom Pilaf (AKA Edith's Pilaf)

a few small mushrooms
1 pinch of saffron
1 mug of basmati rice
2-3 mugs vegetable stock
1 tablespoon olive oil
1 large leek chopped
2 spring onions chopped

Wash the rice several times in cold water until it runs clear. Drain and put into a saucepan with the stock. Bring to boil and simmer for 12 minutes to absorb all liquid, adding more as required. Meanwhile, fry leeks and mushrooms for 3 minutes. When rice is done, add vegetables and heat for a few more moments.

Non! Je ne regrette rien!!

Lemon Dressing

juice of 1 lemon
8 tablespoons olive oil
4 tablespoons light soy sauce
small bunch coriander chopped

Blend lemon juice and soy sauce then the olive oil. Beat until smooth. Add coriander at last moment.

Light Cheese Omelette

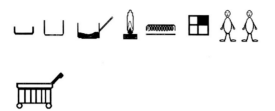

3 eggs, whites and yolks separated
1 knob of butter
½ mug grated cheese
fresh herbs if available
salt and pepper

Beat yolks and seasoning until smooth. Whip whites in a separate container until stiff. Melt butter in the pan, mix whites and yolks and add to pan, cooking slowly for 2-3 minutes until the base is golden. Slide omelette onto heatproof dish and sprinkle most of the cheese on top, fold it over and sprinkle with the rest of the cheese. Put under the grill for 30 seconds or until the cheese is melted. Decorate with fresh herbs such as parsley or basil.

Mediterranean Omelette

6 eggs
1 red or yellow pepper cored and diced
1 courgette finely sliced
1 aubergine finely sliced
1 tomato peeled
1 bunch of coriander
2 knobs butter
olive oil
salt and pepper

Fry vegetables for ten minutes in a little oil, season and add some coriander. Beat eggs with more coriander and seasoning. Cook omelette as normal, adding the filling as the base begins to brown, then fold over and cook for a further 2 minutes.

Mediterranean Toast

6 slices of wholemeal type bread
2 tomatoes
several black olives
2 anchovies (sardines if you prefer)
1 cup of grated cheese
1 - 2 tablespoons olive oil
salt and pepper
sprig of marjoram

Toast bread on both sides. Put a slice of tomato on each. Season and cover with cheese. Add halves of black olives and a few drops of oil. Grill until cheese is melted and turning colour. Garnish with marjoram and a strip of anchovy.

Mexican Leek Salad

2 medium leeks
1 small tin of haricot or red kidney beans
1 large carrot chopped
a few radishes chopped
1 chilli pepper cored and chopped
1 onion chopped
2 pinches of cumin
4 tablespoons grape seed (or olive) oil
2 teaspoons vinegar
1 dessert spoon mustard powder
2 teaspoons of tarragon
2 teaspoons of chervil
2 sprigs mint
1 bunch of spring onions chopped
salt and pepper

Cook leeks and carrots in salt water. Drain, cool, then mix with other vegetables. Blend vinaigrette ingredients and stir well into salad. The herbs may be a problem so substitute.

Mild Tomato Sauce

2 tablespoons olive oil
1 stick celery finely chopped
1 can tomatoes
1 teaspoon sugar
1 teaspoon fresh basil chopped
1 teaspoon parsley chopped
1 small knob butter
salt and pepper

Fry celery and onion until soft. Add rest of ingredients, cover and simmer for 20 minutes. Strain, reheat, add butter and serve with pasta.

Millet Burgers

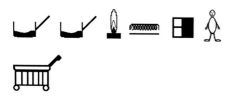

1 mug millet
1 mug vegetable stock
2 tablespoons cooking oil
1 stick celery chopped
1 small onion sliced
½ red or yellow pepper sliced
fresh chopped herbs such as marjoram
½ mug Cheddar grated
salt and pepper

Cook millet in vegetable stock until liquid is absorbed. The millet will be thick. Fry vegetables until soft. Mix all ingredients and shape into burgers. Allow to cool and then grill a few minutes each side until brown.

Eat with a salad.

Mushroom and Rice Salad

2 mugs cooked long grained rice
6 or 8 large mushrooms chopped
1 yellow pepper seeded and chopped
4 tomatoes chopped
2 tablespoon sunflower oil
4 tablespoons mayonnaise
2 teaspoons sweet pepper sauce
salt and pepper

Cook the mushrooms and pepper in the oil for a minute or two,
seasoned with salt and pepper. Mix into the mayonnaise together
with the chopped tomatoes and sweet pepper sauce, then stir into
the rice.

Mustard Sauce

3 tablespoons mustard
2 teaspoons olive oil
1 dash of vinegar
2 tablespoons crème fraîche
salt and pepper

Mix mustard, salt and pepper. Whip up with a little oil at a time and add the vinegar. Whip in the cream gradually.

Great with a crunchy vegetable salad.

Oat Pancakes

1 mug of oats
1 mug oat flour
1 pinch salt
2 eggs
3 teaspoons oil
1 mug milk

Mix oats and flour with salt. In a separate bowl, beat eggs and oil, adding the dry ingredients. Add enough milk to obtain a creamy batter. Heat sufficient oil to cover the base of the pan and pour in 2-3 tablespoons of batter to form a thin layer. Cook gently until bubbles form. Turn with spatula or tosss if you dare! Cook for 30 seconds on other side. Eat with sweet or savoury accompaniment.

Olive and Anchovy Dressing

1 carton yogourt
½ mug green or black olives pitted and finely chopped
1 clove garlic crushed
2 anchovies thinly sliced and chopped
1 tablespoon olive oil
1 teaspoon sweet pepper sauce
pepper

Blend all ingredients. Serve with salad.

Omelette Sandwich

2 eggs
2 tomatoes
watercress
2 knobs butter
a small quantiity of vegetarian "bacon bits"
French loaf
salt and pepper

Cut the bread lengthwise and butter. Beat eggs with a teaspoon or two of water and cook in hot butter until just runny in the centre. Fold the omelette so that the one edge meets the middle and then sprinkle the uncovered half with "bacon bits" or crushed salted nuts and fold over. Place on half the loaf and garnish with tomato and watercress. It can be eaten cold if you are planning a walk. Wrap in foil or clingfilm.

Omelette with Garlic Cubits

3 eggs
2 cloves of garlic crushed
3 teaspoons oil
1 knob of butter
1 slice of white bread crusts removed and cubed
salt and pepper

Fry the garlic in the butter and oil mixture for a few seconds and then add the bread cubes, cooking until golden. Dry on kitchen paper and cook the omelette, folding in the cubes at the appropriate moment. Eat with a salad.

Orange Salad

1 curly lettuce or similar
1 bunch parsley chopped
1 bunch mint chopped
1 orange chopped and juice saved
a few strips of orange peel pithless and finely chopped
1 handful raisins and sultanas
1 teaspoon lime juice
2 tablespoons grapefruit juice
2 tablespoons olive oil
salt and pepper

Mix all ingredients and season just before serving.

Orange Watercress and Leek Salad

1 bunch watercress chopped
1 small orange chopped and juice saved
1 leek chopped
1 handful salted peanuts
2 tablespoons sunflower oil
salt and pepper

Mix ingredients and season.

Crouton garnish. Fry small cubes of bread in hot oil to which a couple of cloves of crushed garlic have been added. Sprinkle at once onto salad.

Pan Fried Mushrooms

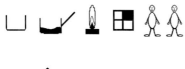

6-8 large flat (field) mushrooms
3 tablespoons groundnut oil
1 knob butter
3 shallots chopped
oregano and basil
spring onions
parsley
salt and pepper

Separate stalks from heads and wipe on kitchen towel. Cook in oil until water contained in mushrooms has evaporated. Drain. Heat butter until it darkens and then add mushrooms and shallots. Fry until cooked and then turn out onto a plate, season and add spring onions with herbs.

Parsnip Soup

2 large parsnips
1 large onion
1 carrot
½ mug Parmesan
2 teaspoons mixed herbs
1 tablespoon Worcestershire sauce
celery leaves
3 mugs vegetable stock
1 teaspoon plum sauce
salt and pepper

Chop the vegetables very finely, add other ingredients, stir well, bring to boil, cover and simmer for ½ hour.

Pasta Spirals and Avocado Salad

sufficient cooked pasta spirals for 2 people (see pack)
2 tablespoons olive oil with crushed garlic
1 very ripe avocado mashed
1 tablespoon sun dried tomatoes in olive oil
1 teaspoon pesto
1 teaspoon Worcestershire sauce
1 teaspoon light soy sauce
1 small chicory chopped
black pepper

Mix all ingredients with the pasta and sprinkle with black pepper.

Peasant Frittata

2 eggs
1 small courgette diced
1 small stick celery chopped
2 tablespoons oil
1 tomato chopped
1 tablespoon Parmesan
1 teaspoon fresh basil chopped
salt and pepper

Fry celery in half the oil over low heat for 5 minutes. Add courgette, tomato and seasoning and cook very gently for a further few minutes, stirring occasionally. Beat eggs, cheese and basil, add rest of oil to pan and heat for a minute. Cook eggs for 4 minutes, turn over and cook for a further 4 minutes. Cut and sprinkle with more Parmesan

Pepper Grill

1 large red pepper grilled or boiled and sliced
1 large yellow pepper ditto
4 tablespoons olive oil
2 garlic cloves crushed
2 anchovies chopped
4 black olives chopped
3 teaspoons capers
spaghetti for 2 people already cooked if possible
3 teaspoons breadcrumbs
3 tablespoons Parmesan

Fry peppers with garlic for a couple of minutes. Add anchovies, olives, capers and seasoning. Cook spaghetti and drain, (or use pre-cooked pasta), adding some oil. Mix a little oil, bread crumbs and Parmesan and use half to cover the pasta in a heatproof dish. Layer with half the peppers and finish off with the remainder of the cheese and breadcrumbs mixture. Grill until cheese is golden and crisp.

If you have no capers, don't worry!

Peppers, Eggs and Potatoes

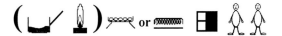

2 red or yellow peppers
2 hard boiled eggs chopped
2 mugs cooked potato mash
2 tablespoons mayonnaise
1 teaspoon mustard
2 spring onions finely chopped
1 teaspoon paprika
½ teaspoon garlic salt (or make your own)*
pepper
parsley

Cut a circular "lid" around the stalk off the top of each pepper and with the fingers, extract carefully the pith and seeds. Mix the eggs and potato and blend in the mayonnaise, onions, mustard, garlic salt and pepper. Fill peppers carefully with spoonsful of the mixture.

Wrap them separately in doubled foil and cook under a grill or on a barbecue for about 30 minutes, turning occasionally.

*Crush garlic with a little salt

69

Pineapple Sauce

1 teaspoon paprika
4 tablespoons mayonnaise
1 segment lemon
2 slices of pineapple finely chopped
2 teaspoons honey
salt and pepper

Crush the pineapple and squeeze lemon juice over it. Mix rest of ingredients.

Great with salad or fish dishes.

Pinto Beans in Tomato Sauce

1 can pinto beans
1 bay leaf
2 tablespoons olive oil
1 onion chopped
2 cloves garlic crushed
1 teaspoon chopped fresh sage
2 large tomatoes chopped
1 teaspoon balsamic vinegar
1 teaspoon parsley chopped
salt and pepper

Drain beans and pour on enough cold fresh water to cover.
Bring to boil and remove from heat. Meanwhile, fry onion, sage
and garlic until soft. Add tomatoes, bay leaf, a couple of
tablepoons water and the vinegar.

Cook for another 5 minutes. Add drained beans to the mixture
and simmer for a further 5 minutes. Season and add parsley.

Pistou Soup

1 small can kidney beans drained
3 tablespoons olive oil
1 stick celery chopped
1 onion chopped
2 potatoes diced
1 branch of broccoli chopped
2 carrots chopped
1 courgette chopped
2 tomatoes chopped
1 mug macaroni
1 bunch parsley chopped
2 sprigs basil chopped
2 tablespoons pine nuts
½ mug Parmesan
2 cloves of garlic crushed
salt and pepper

Fry vegetables until soft, add macaroni, cover with water and simmer for 45 minutes. Crush garlic, basil, Parmesan and nuts in a little oil. Add mixture at last minute to soup.

Potato and Herb Omelette

3 eggs
1 large potato cooked and finely chopped
1 teaspoon fresh rosemary
1 teaspoon chervil
salt and pepper

Fry potato pieces until golden and crunchy. Dry on kitchen paper and then mix with herbs. Make the omelette as usual and fill with the mixture.

This recipe is useful if you have leftover potato from the previous day.

Potato Pancake Sauce

1 knob of butter
1 onion chopped
1 can tomatoes
1 teaspoon sugar
3 teaspoons Worcestershire sauce
3 hard boiled eggs chopped
salt and pepper

Fry onion for 5 minutes over low heat. Add tomatoes in juice, seasoning, sugar and sauce. Simmer for 10 minutes to enable mixture to thicken a little. Add eggs to mixture and simmer for 2 minutes stirring meanwhile. Serve hot on savoury pancakes.

Potato Pancakes

2 large potatoes
1 mug of flour
2 eggs
1 mug milk
oil
salt and pepper

Boil potatoes for 10 minutes, chop finely, add flour and mix. Beat eggs and milk and stir gradually into potatoes. Season. Pour 4 - 6 tablespoons of mixture into heated pan and cook both sides.

Prawn Curry

1 can prawns drained
1 small can pineapple chunks
1 carrot
1 stick celery
1 handful of mushrooms
1 onion
1 small courgette
1 small apple
½ red pepper
all the vegetables above chopped small
vegetable stock (stock cube plus pineapple juice)
vegetable oil
4 cloves garlic crushed
2 tablespoons mango chutney
curry powder to taste

If time is available, marinate prawns in a mixture of curry powder and a little stock. Fry all vegetables and fruit until soft, add stock and prawns, bring to boil and simmer for 30 minutes. Serve with boiled rice.

Provencal Fennel

2 fennel roots cut lengthwise in 1cm slices
3 tablespoons olive oil
4 cloves of garlic crushed
6 large tomatoes chopped
1 mug of white wine
a few black olives
2 sprigs of thyme
2 bay leaves
1 pinch of sugar
salt and pepper

Fry fennel each side for 5 minutes until golden. Put aside and add tomatoes and wine to the pan and boil vigorously for 5 minutes. Add olives, herbs and sugar. Put back the fennel, cover and simmer for 20 minutes, season and serve hot, cold or at room temperature as preferred.

Quorn on the Hob

1 pack of quorn sausages
1 can of tomatoes in juice
1 tablespoon tomato paste
1 tablespoon of prepared pesto
1 tablespoon Worcestershire sauce
1 teaspoon mustard
2 teaspoons honey
salt and pepper

Cook the sausages according to the instructions on the packet. Then add them to the other already mixed ingredients and heat for 10 minutes over a low flame. Eat with rice or noodles

Red Pepper Sauce

1 red pepper chopped
1 very ripe tomato chopped
1 clove garlic crushed
1 tablespoon vegetable stock
1 sprig of basil chopped
½ chilli pepper chopped
1 sprig thyme chopped
1 tablespoon olive oil
½ mug tomato sauce
salt

Fry the tomato, garlic and peppers until soft, add stock and tomato sauce and bring back to boil. Simmer gently for a couple of minutes. Season, stir and allow to cool if wished or use hot on freshly cooked vegetables.

Red Salmon Salad

1 can red salmon
1 curly lettuce or similar
1 bunch parsley chopped
1 bunch mint chopped
2 tablespoons olive oil
2-3 teaspoons white wine vinegar
2-3 strips anchovy chopped finely
1 very ripe avocado mashed
pepper

Break up the salmon roughly with a fork. Mix the avocado,
pepper and anchovy into a creamy paste and fork into the salmon.

Rice and Peanut Fry

1 mug long grained rice
1 egg beaten
a handful of beansprouts
1 handful of peanuts crushed
1 tablespoon sunflower oil
1 tablespoon light soy sauce
pepper

Cook the rice and wash in hot water. Drain well and fry with peanuts and beansprouts for a few minutes. Add soy sauce to mixture and stir. Continue heating whilst dribbling the egg into the hot mixture. Fry until beginning to turn golden.

Ricotta Pancakes

For Batter:
½ mug wholemeal flour
1-2 eggs
1 mug milk
1 pinch of salt

For Filling:
1 small carton of ricotta
3 teaspoons Parmesan
2 teaspoons marjoram
1 knob of butter
2 tablespoons flour
3 teaspoons tomato paste
½ mug vegetable stock

Beat ricotta, Parmesan, marjoram, salt and pepper until creamy.
Make the pancakes, fill them and fold in 4. Melt butter in
heatproof dish and stir in flour. Add stock and tomato paste.
Season and add pancakes. Spoon liquid over them and put under
hot grill for 2 minutes.

Roast Curried Parsnips

2 medium parsnips
aluminium foil
2 cloves garlic sliced into thin slivers
light soy sauce
2 tablespoons olive oil or similar vegetable oil
curry powder

Cut small slits in the parsnips and insert slivers of garlic. Pour a little oil and soy sauce over each parsnip and roll in the mixture. (The parsnips, not yourself!) Dust well with curry powder until covered. Wrap in foil and seal well. Bake on embers or under grill until cooked.

Variations:

This recipe can be used for leeks, carrots or whole smallish onions.

Savoury Mashed Potato

mashed potato from Crunchy Potato Peel recipe
1 knob butter
1 mug grated Cheddar
1 tomato sliced
salt and pepper

Blend butter into mash and cover with grated cheese in a
heatproof dish. Put slices of tomato on top and grill for several
minutes until cheese is melted.

Savoury Pancakes

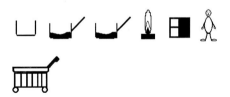

For Batter:
½ mug wholemeal flour
1-2 eggs
1 mug milk
pinch of salt

For Filling:
1 knob butter or margarine
1 medium onion finely chopped
1 mug mushrooms finely chopped
2 large tomatoes finely chopped
soya bacon bits
small tin soya sausages
tomato sauce for serving (See page 95)

Beat together all batter ingredients and put aside. Add more milk
if very thick. Cook vegetables in a second pan in hot oil until soft.
Add bacon bits and sausages. Put aside but keep warm if you
can. Heat a little butter in pan and add some pancake mixture,
spreading evenly. Cook until light brown and then flip or turn with
knife. Remove from pan and roll with filling inside.
Eat with salad

Savoury Rice

½ - ¾ mug rice
2-3 tablespoons olive oil
2 small onions
1 red pepper finely chopped
1 litre vegetable stock
salt and black pepper

Fry the vegetables until beginning to soften, add rice and cook
until transparent. Add boiling stock spoon by spoon until absorbed.
Continue cooking until rice is done - about 15 minutes.

Spicy Yogourt Dressing

1 carton yogourt
1 teaspoon groundnut oil
½ teaspoon paprika
1 pinch curry powder
1 teaspoon cumin
1 cardamom
1 teaspoon lemon juice
2 teaspoons coriander chopped
1 teaspoon ground ginger
1 teaspoon mustard
salt

Mix thoroughly.

Stuffed Aubergine

2 small aubergines
1 knob of butter
1 onion finely chopped
2 cloves garlic finely chopped
1 can tomatoes
1 mug of breadcrumbs
1 mug grated Cheddar
1 teaspoon oregano
salt and pepper
aluminium foil

Cut a horizontal "lid " around the aubergines and hollow out top
and bottom, leaving a "wall" about 0.5cm thick. Chop the flesh
finely. Cook garlic and onion until soft. Add the aubergine flesh
and cook again until soft. Reduce heat and add mixture of
breadcrumbs, cheese and oregano. Season. Stuff the aubergines
and replace the lids. Wrap separately in a double layer of foil and
cook on barbecue for 20-30 minutes.

Sweet and Sour Aubergine

1 aubergine peeled and cubed for kebabs
1 tablespoon sugar
1 pinch of cayenne pepper
1 small sprig marjoram chopped
1 tablespoon parsley chopped
1 teaspoon mustard
1 clove garlic crushed
1 tablespoon olive oil
2 teaspoons tarragon
salt and pepper

Mix all ingredients apart from marjoram. Put aside for 15 minutes, stirring occasionally. Thread aubergine on kebab sticks and grill or barbecue for 15 minutes

Sweet and Sour Sauce

1 tablespoon grilled chopped almonds
1 tablespoon raisins or sultanas
4 tablespoons groundnut oil
juice of 1 orange
1 clove garlic crushed
1 slice of orange peel, pith removed, chopped finely
1 teaspoon honey
salt and pepper

Heat honey, pour in orange juice and bring to boil. Add raisins, garlic and seasoning. Allow to cool. Beat in oil. Boil orange peel in a little water and add with almonds to the mixture.

Tasty with fish.

Sweet Peppers with Anchovies

2 red or yellow peppers
8 or so black olives
2 strips of salted anchovy
1 tablespoon red wine
olive oil
1 pot of capers
oregano
1 mug cold cooked rice
aluminium foil
pepper

Cut peppers in two and stuff with mixture of olives, capers,
anchovy, a pinch of oregano and a dash of red wine. Wrap in foil
and boil in water for 20 minutes or so or until peppers are done.

Tartare Vegetables

a few cauliflower florets
2 large carrots chopped
1 stick celery chopped
1 bunch radishes chopped
some white cabbage shredded
2 tomatoes chopped
a quantity of cucumber sliced

Dressing
1 tablespoon of groundnut oil
½ teaspoon paprika
1 teaspoon curry powder
1 teaspoon cumin
1 teaspoon lemon juice
1 teaspoon chopped coriander
1 teaspoon ginger
1 teaspoon mustard
1 small pot yogourt
salt

Mix dressing ingredients. Serve sauce separate from salad
vegetables.

Thai Noodles

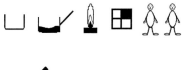

2 sheets of Chinese noodles
1 small chilli pepper seeded and finely chopped
1 tablespoon crunchy peanut butter
2 teaspoons lime juice
1 tablespoon sunflower oil
1 clove garlic crushed
1 tablespoon light soy sauce

Cook the noodles according to the instructions on the packet. In the mean time make the dressing by mixing the oil, garlic and peanut butter until smooth. Add the chilli, soy sauce and lime juice and season to taste. Drain the noodles, add the dressing and toss well.

Tomato and Peanut Grill

2 large tomatoes halved
Worcestershire sauce
1 teaspoon fresh basil chopped
1 teaspoon fresh parsley chopped
1 to 2 tablespoons Parmesan
1 handful of roast peanut crushed
1 knob butter
6 rounds of French loaf fried
pepper

Season the cut side of the tomatoes with pepper and sprinkle a
few drops of Worcestershire sauce. Cover with a mixture of basil,
parsley, Parmesan and chopped peanuts. Add a small knob of
butter to each one. Place each tomato on kitchen foil, cut side up,
and grill or barbecue for 20-25 minutes. Remove and serve on a
round of fried bread.

Tomato Sauce

2 tablespoons cooking oil
1 smallish onion chopped
1 clove garlic crushed
1 level tablespoon wholemeal flour
6-8 tomatoes chopped
parsley chopped
2 tablespoons tomato paste
1 tablespoon prepared pesto
salt and pepper

Fry vegetables until soft and then add flour, cooking for ½ minute or so. Add water, tomato paste and parsley, stir well, season to taste and simmer for 20-30 minutes. Sieve if you have the means and want to do so, but it always seems a pity!

Variations:

Leeks instead of onions. Tinned tomatoes instead of fresh, or fresh basil or any other herb you may have or prefer.

Tuna Dressing

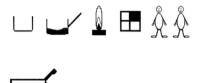

1 can tuna in oil chopped
2 sprigs of parsley
1 clove garlic crushed
2 teaspoons wine, red or white
½ mug tomato sauce
2 aubergines diced
pepper

Fry the aubergines in a little of the oil drained from the tuna with
the garlic. When the aubergine is beginning to turn dark brown,
add wine and sprinkle with parsley. Put aside.

Fry the tuna over high flame in its own oil, add tomato sauce,
bring to the boil, mix with other ingredients and cook for 2-3
minutes.

Vegetable and Fruit Curry

curry powder to taste
1 large onion chopped
2 carrots diced
2 potatoes diced small
1 teaspoon ground ginger
4 very ripe tomatoes chopped
1-2 mugs vegetable stock
1 cup of defrosted peas
1 apple cored and chopped
1 small mango chopped or 3 tablespoons mango chutney
a small handful of cashew or pistachio nuts chopped
1 tablespoon desiccated coconut
1-2 teaspoons coriander
2 cloves garlic crushed
1 tablespoon garam masala
olive oil

Fry all the vegetables gently in a little oil for a couple of minutes, stirring constantly, then add stock and remainder of ingredients. Simmer for 20 minutes and add garam masala at the end to thicken and enhance flavour.

Vegetable Curry

1 large carrot
1 stick celery
a handful of mushrooms
1 onion
1 parsnip
1 small courgette
1 small apple
1 small potato
½ red pepper
all the above chopped small

1 can haricot, pinto or kidney beans, drained and rinsed
1 small handful raisins and sultanas
vegetable stock
vegetable oil
4 cloves garlic crushed
2 tablespoons mango chutney
curry powder to taste

Fry ingredients apart from chutney in a little oil for 5 minutes, add
1-2 tablespoons flour and curry powder, fry for a couple of
minutes then add stock and chutney, bring to boil and simmer for 1
hour. Serve with boiled rice if required.

Vegetable Mayonnaise

2 tablespoons mayonnaise
1 onion cooked and chopped
1 carrot cooked but still crunchy, chopped
a few drops of tabasco or chilli sauce
1 tablespoon spring onion chopped
1 dash of vinegar
salt and pepper

Mix well. Add vinegar just before serving.

White Cheese Sauce

1 small carton of cream cheese
1 bunch of spring onions chopped
2 teaspoons of tarragon
2 teaspoons of chervil
3 leaves of mint chopped
2 tomatoes chopped
1 tablespoon lemon juice
salt and pepper

Mix all ingredients well.

From the same Publisher:

Camping and Caravanning in France
The "Survival" Guide
by Rick Allen

ISBN   0 9533386 0 6

The Guide for the motorist, biker, backpacker, cyclist, camper,
caravanner and motorcaravanner or the ordinary traveller in
France, French speaker or not

Price £9.99 including postage to purchasers of
either

Movable Feast or *Movable Bean Feasts*

Offer applicable only to mail order purchases direct from the
Publisher

Editions de la Montagne
PO Box 732
Southampton
SO16 7RQ
UK

Bookshop price normally £12.50

Movable Feasts

ISBN 0 9533386 1 4

The companion volume to *Movable Bean Feasts*, but this time **mainly for meat eaters**.

Again, there are over 100 easy but often unusual recipes for people on the move, on holiday or in accommodation where facilities may be limited.

The book is down to earth, practical and fun as you would expect from this no-nonsense author.

Order it from your local bookshop
or direct from the Publishers £6.99 plus postage and packing £1.25

Editions de la
Montagne

PO Box   732
Southampton
SO16 7RQ
England

Notes

Notes